MAKING THE GRADE

THE TEEN'S GUIDE TO HOMEWORK SUCCESS

by
Janice Gabe, LCSW, MAC

Professional Resource Publications
Indianapolis, IN

Published by
Professional Resource Publications
P.O. Box 501485
Indianapolis, IN 46256
www.newperspectives-indy.com

ISBN: 0-9639023-1-8

Publisher's Cataloging-in-Publication Data

DEDICATION

*To the hundreds of young people who have
enriched my life sharing their lives, their struggles,
their joys and their problems with me.*

*To my favorite kid in the world,
my incredible son Kyle.*

*To my husband Steve
for his support and encouragement.*

TABLE OF CONTENTS

FORWARD

TO TEENS

I imagine that this book came into your possession because some well meaning adult is worried about your grades and is desperately searching for something to help you or motivate you. If that is the case, you are probably looking for the same thing, but certainly don't want anyone to know it.

I have talked to hundreds of teens about the problems they have with doing their homework. With their help, I have discovered some things that really will make it easier for you. I tried to keep this book simple, short, not too boring and most importantly of all, realistic. So, spend a few minutes and read it. What do you have to lose?

TO PARENTS

I was recently sitting in my office, trying to catch up on paperwork when I received a call from a mother of one of my clients. This client was an adolescent male who was referred to me because he struggled in school. The mom was calling to let me know that report cards had come out. Of course I knew this because all adolescent therapists are aware when report cards come out. They know phones will begin ringing off the hook. The next few minutes provided me with a rewarding conversation in which the mother informed me that her son's grades had gotten dramatically better and she just wanted to let me know and to thank me. Of course the one who was responsible for changing her son's grades was her son. I just helped him find a little motivation.

No sooner had I hung up the phone when I received another call from another set of parents. They explained they called me because they heard I helped kids who had school problems. After I finished the call, I began to reflect on the hundreds of conversations I have had with teens over the years about schoolwork. I realized that most of these teens shared common themes and, that while they were all individuals, the solutions to their problems were similar. That is what inspired me to write this book to share with teens what I have learned from teens over the years.

One of the primary purposes of this book is to encourage teens to take responsibility for their schoolwork. In order to accomplish this, please allow them to read this book and decide what, if any, strategies in it will be helpful to them. Please do not read this book for them and suggest strategies. Please do not ask them if they have read it, what they got out of it, or what they plan to do. Teens often resist doing their schoolwork because they are locked into a power struggle with their parents. This book cannot help them if it becomes part of that power struggle.

What can I do you ask? By all means, I would encourage you to read this book. It is my hope that it will provide you with some valuable insight into what is actually happening when it comes to your teen and his or her homework. I hope that you find *Chapter Six, A Word for Parents,* particularly helpful.

TO PROFESSIONALS

I have attempted to write a practical, realistic and useful book for teens. You will find that they can easily read it themselves in a very short time and understand the advice offered. However, the book would serve very effectively as a discussion guide for a group or classroom and I would encourage you to use it as such.

CHAPTER ONE

Don't Tell Me You Don't Care

I am an adolescent therapist who has talked to hundreds of adolescents over the last twenty years. Everything I know about adolescents, I learned from listening to teens. Over the years I have talked to many young people who have been brought to my office (often against their will) because their parents are concerned about the adolescents' grades.

"They just don't seem to care," the parents exclaim.

"How do you know this?" I ask.

"Because if they cared, their grades would be better," parents respond.

So I ask the teens.

"What do you think about your grades?" I ask.
"I think they could be better," you tell me.
"So why aren't they?" I question.

This is where the fun begins. This is were we find out what is really going on with your grades. But whatever your answer to this question, please don't tell me you don't care. Why do I not want to hear this? Because it is simply not true.

"I don't care" is something you tell adults to make them crazy. It works, it does make adults crazy. Good for you that you figured that out. However, it does not do much to solve your problem with your grades.

That's right, it is your problem.
Not your parents' problem.

I have talked to hundreds of teens and almost as many young children. I have learned over the years that when kids start first or second grade, they all want to get straight A's. They all care. So what happens? What has happened to you?

This is what we need to find out.

I really do not believe that kids start school with the goal of failure. I do not believe that kids start middle school or high school with the goal of making poor grades.

I know you tell yourself and others that "I could do it if I tried, I just don't try."

Maybe this is true, maybe it is not. This is, however, irrelevant because if you are not trying and your grades are poor, what's the difference? The end result is that your grades are poor and that is not a good situation for you. So the issue is not that you could do it if you tried. The issue is if you are not trying, why not?

I believe that most kids want to do better in school. The entire purpose of this book is to help you accomplish that.

I have worked with many kids around the concepts in this book. If you read this book (don't worry, it's pretty short) and use the things we discuss, your grades will get better.

So don't tell me you don't care.

Get real with yourself.

You know and I know that deep down inside you do care but you might be a little bit afraid. It is easier to not try and use that as an excuse for your failure than it is to try and fail. Don't be afraid, there is a better option and all you have to do is read on.

CHAPTER TWO

Homework—It's Got to Happen

If you are going to have any success at school, you have to do your homework

I know that this is a reality that you do not like, but it is nonetheless true. Let's face it, you have already tried to succeed without doing your home-work, and it has not worked. If you could have made it work, I am sure you would have. After all, you are a bright kid.

I know, I know. You know a guy who gets straight A's and he never studies. But obviously that is not you or you would not be reading this book. So that particular technique is not going to work for you. If it is any comfort, I know many kids who get straight A's and the funny thing is, they all study.

Of course some of them think it's pretty cool to tell everyone they don't study.

So, if you have to do your homework to get your grades up (and you do), let's talk about what you do that makes doing your homework more difficult than it needs to be.

CONNING YOURSELF

How many times have you brought your books home with every intention of studying only to discover that once you got home, you did not really want to study?

This is where the con game begins.

You don't want to study, but you don't want to admit to yourself that you don't want to study, so you start conning yourself.

Does this sound familiar to you?

—"I've been at school all day. I don't want to study now. I'll just watch TV (talk on the phone, check my e-mail, whatever, whatever, whatever). When I am done with that, I'll study."

—"It's too late to start on anything now, I will just wait until after dinner."

—"Now my favorite show is on, I'll do it after Dawson's Creek. I do better under pressure."

—"I'm too tired to do it now. I'll just get up early in the morning and do it."

—"I don't feel like getting up so early. I'll just do it on the bus (in the car, on the way to school, whatever, whatever)."

—"I can't concentrate in the car, I'll just do my English during math class."

—"Oh screw it. It's just one assignment, it won't hurt me that much to miss it. I'll just make sure I do it next time."

—"Well it's too late now, this nine weeks is wasted, I'll do better next grading period."

—"Oh well, I'm just a freshman. I still have three more years to pull up my GPA."

The funny thing about the hundreds of conversations I have had with kids over the years about homework is that I never met a student who told me. "I am a rotten student and plan to continue to be." Most of them tell me, "I'm getting ready to get serious and do it differently."

So, let's talk about this con game you run on yourself. The reason you con yourself is to give yourself an excuse to put off doing your homework. I would venture to say that most of the time you don't do your work after talking on the phone, after watching TV, after getting on line and most definitely you are not going to get up in the morning to do your work. So if you are not going to do your work, at least get honest with yourself.

*Stop making excuses.
Try some reality.
Try telling yourself the truth.*

"I am just conning myself again."

"I always say I'm going to do it later, and I never do."

"I know I am not going to get up in the morning to do this work."

"I know that every time I miss an assignment, I am digging myself deeper into a hole that is hard to climb out of."

"When I choose not to do my work, I am choosing the consequences that go with that."

Conning yourself makes it easy to continue to avoid dealing with your homework. When you tell yourself the truth, it makes it harder to avoid putting off what you need to do.

MAKING IT WORSE THAN IT HAS TO BE

Okay, so homework is not the most exciting activity around. I can't argue with that. It's just one of those things that you have to do. You don't make this task any easier on yourself by convincing yourself the task is actually worse than it is.

Do you ever find yourself thinking this way about your homework?

—"I hate homework!!"

—"Homework is stupid!"

—"Homework is boring!"

—"I just can't do it. I can't stand it."

Well, by the time you are done thinking about it, you would be an idiot to make yourself tackle such an unpleasant task. By thinking so negatively about your homework, you talk yourself out of doing it. You make it much worse than it has to be. So, if you want homework to seem like a more manageable thing for you, you have to start thinking about it differently.

The truth about homework is this.

- —"There are things I would rather do, but it's not that boring."

- —"I don't like it, but I can put up with it."

- —"Homework is something everyone has to do, and everyone does, so I can manage it."

"It only makes it worse when I sit around thinking about how bad it is, I might as well do it and get it out of the way."

CONVINCING YOURSELF IT'S TOO MUCH

Sometimes, in an attempt to help kids with their homework, parents make the mistake of saying, "That's it! From now on you are going to study two hours a night at the kitchen table where I can watch you."

This, as you know does not usually help. In fact, sometimes it makes the situation worse because it promotes the attitude that if you are going to do better in school, you are going to have to study all the time. It's very difficult to go from not studying at all to studying several hours a night.

Many teens do not study at all because they know that if they wanted to get all A's, they would probably have to study for many hours every night (unless of course you're one of those genius kids which most of us are not).

Some kids who are poor students, are not kids who do not care. In fact, they are kids who want to be perfect.

They know that to get perfect grades they would have to study an unbelievable amount of hours. They know they probably won't study that much, so they just do not study at all.

So, it is true that to get all A's, you probably have to put in a lot of hours.

However, all A's does not have to be your goal.

The truth is, that if you study just a little more than you are studying now, your grades will probably go up a letter grade.

So while you may not be willing to study for several hours more a night, you might be willing to study for 30 or 60 minutes more a night. Now that's more like it. That's more realistic, and that is surely something you can talk yourself into.

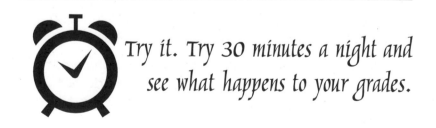

Try it. Try 30 minutes a night and see what happens to your grades.

We know one thing for sure. They won't get any worse.

CONVINCING YOURSELF THAT HOMEWORK DOES NOT MATTER

There are many reasons why people get poor grades. I have discovered that the number one reason for most students is that they do not turn in their homework.

It is easy to convince yourself that your homework does not matter.

But you know what, it really does matter.

—Most students find that they can raise their grades significantly simply by turning in their homework assignments.

—You have already discovered that NOT turning in your assignments, really hurts your grades.

—If you do your homework, you will be somewhat prepared for tests and quizzes. If you do not do your homework, you won't be prepared for tests and quizzes.

Turn in your assignments. Try it for a grading period just to see what a difference it will make.

CHAPTER THREE

But I don't Want to Go to College (and Other Lame Excuses)

There are a lot of excuses students make to justify their poor grades. The sad thing is that many students do not even believe these excuses, but they get so used to them that it is hard to let them go. Let's take a look at some of these and see if you recognize yourself.

BUT I DON'T WANT TO GO TO COLLEGE

Many students use "I don't want to go to college," as an excuse and justification for not doing their homework. It is a lame excuse all the way around, and we will talk a lot about that in this chapter.

For now let's focus on this concept that you don't want to go to college. (Now here's the good news, if you don't use this as an excuse, you don't have to read this section.)

I always find it fascinating when teens tell me they do not want to go to college because they hate school and are sick of school. I find it especially interesting because I said that myself during my freshman year of high school. Not only did I end up going to college, but I went to college for a long time.

The truth is, not everyone is cut out for college. Not everyone will go and not everyone should go. So I do not have a problem with students saying I'm not going to college.

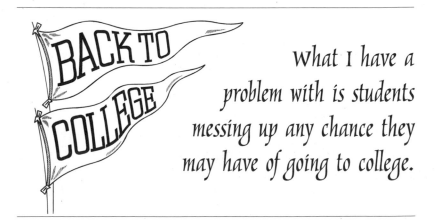

What I have a problem with is students messing up any chance they may have of going to college.

Think back on your life. When you were a little kid in kindergarten, what did you want to do when you grew up? Did you want to be a policeman, a nurse, a ballerina? What about when you were a little older, in third grade. Did you want to be a doctor, a mechanic, a football player? What about in fifth grade? Did you want to be scientist, a marine biologist, a teacher? What about middle school?

The point is, as you grow and mature you go through many phases and many different changes. That is normal. What you want to be today, may not require college. What you want to be next year may not require college. But it might.

The most important thing is to keep your options open.

Keep your grades up so that all doors are open to you.

Not knowing what you want to do after high school is not necessarily the same as not wanting to go to college. Try to remember this.

It makes me sad when I talk to students who realize (sometimes too late) that they have changed their mind and really do want to go to college. It makes me even sadder because I talk to a lot of these individuals. They always regret their earlier decisions to blow off school. I have never met an older teen or young adult who says, "I am really glad I messed around in school and ruined my grades. I would make that decision again if I had a second chance." I do often hear, "Man, it would have been so easy to just do my homework, I can't believe I was so stupid."

Matt was a very bright and artistically talented client of mine. He always did well in art classes but was not interested in his traditional classes. He could have done the work, but could not find a reason to motivate himself and I certainly could not find the motivation for him. In addition to lack of interest, Matt did not like the way high school was conducted and was often in conflict with teachers. Once he got mad at a teacher, he would refuse to work in that teacher's class.

As I got to know Matt, I worried about him because I knew he was the kind of person who would not be happy with himself unless he was able to accomplish something with his life. During his senior year he went to visit a relative out of state and also visited a graphic design college. For the first time in his adolescence, he felt like he belonged. He loved the campus. He was enthusiastic about the curriculum. He met and liked the instructors. He finally knew what he wanted to do.

Unfortunately, he could not take action because his grades were not good enough to get in.

All those teachers on whom he sought revenge by not doing his homework, and the school against which he rebelled, were totally unaffected by his grades. He, on the other hand, was greatly hurt.

BUT I'M JUST A FRESHMAN, I HAVE PLENTY OF TIME TO GET MY GRADES UP

Many students who get poor grades really do plan to attend college after high school. They fully intend to get their grades up eventually and feel it is not necessary to do it now. There are several problems with this type of thinking.

To begin with, now that you're a freshman, your grades do count.

The grades you make during your freshman and sophomore year will impact your overall GPA.

When you are a junior (which is the time that most students get concerned about their grades) you will have to deal with the negative impact that two years of poor school performance has had on your grades. It takes a tremendous amount of effort to get grades that are good enough to bring up one or two years of poor grades.

I often discuss this topic with students who are freshmen and sophomores.

I jokingly tell them I don't want to have to listen to them when they are juniors tell me how much they regret their earlier decisions.

I AM A SMART KID, I CAN GET MY GRADES UP ANYTIME I WANT

I have no doubt that you are a smart kid and that you are capable of getting your grades up. However, I am concerned that it will not be quite as easy as you think.

Learning how to study is a skill. It is like any other skill, it requires practice. You may be a gifted athlete and have a lot of natural ability.

However, you cannot pick up a basketball one day and play competitive ball the next.

You have to develop your skill. You develop it by working and practicing. The same is true for studying and using your brain. You may be extremely bright, but if you have not learned to study, it will take time for you to learn those skills. The sooner you start the better.

28

If you are an athlete who has not practiced your sport for a while, you know what it is like to get back into shape. You struggle, you're sore, it's a lot of work to get back into shape. The same thing goes for study skills. It is a lot of work and takes some time to get back into good study habits. Because it does take time, you really cannot afford to wait very long.

I once had a very bright middle school kid tell me that he did not care about his grades in middle school because they did not really count. He assured me that once he got to high school, he would get serious about his grades. No matter what anyone did, he refused to take middle school seriously. When he moved into his freshman year he promised himself and everyone else that he would really get focused and work hard in school. He was very upset to discover that several things happened to him during his "lazy period" in middle school. He discovered that studying was very hard for him because he was out of practice. He also discovered that although he was bright, he was really struggling with his schoolwork. There were several things he did not understand. What he realized is that school is based on a building block process.

In order to do well tomorrow, you have to learn what you are being taught today.

So this very bright student discovered he had missed out on many things in middle school that he needed to know in order to perform well in high school. As a result of his experience, he began to think maybe he was not so smart after all.

You have to decide when you plan to use that brain of yours. The longer you wait, the more difficult it is going to be.

BUT I AM NEVER GOING TO USE ALGEBRA AGAIN

Actually, I was a terrible math student and I can honestly say that after my freshman year of college I never used algebra again. I might actually have occasion to use it, but I never understood it enough to put it to practical use. I do not disagree with you. You may never use some of the things you are currently learning in school. But whether or not you will use them is really not the issue in learning them. You learn algebra (English, history, whatever, whatever) for an entirely different reason.

The point of learning algebra is not learning algebra.

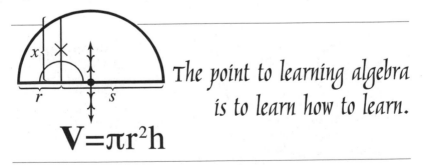

The point to learning algebra is to learn how to learn.

$$V = \pi r^2 h$$

There is a certain part of your brain that can only grow and develop when it is exposed to math.

There is a certain part of your brain that can only grow when it is exposed to grammar. There is a certain part of your brain that can only grow when it is exposed to foreign language.

So in order to access that part of your brain you have to expose it to things that will help it develop.

You may never need algebra, but you will certainly need some skill that lives in that part of the brain. So even if you hate the subject, are not good at the subject, never plan to use the subject again, you still need to put effort into learning the subject.

Perhaps algebra (or Shakespeare, or grammar) has a place in our lives to teach us how to focus and tackle tasks we do not necessarily like. No matter what you choose to do as a career, there will be tasks that you do not like. So you have to learn to put effort into things that are hard, things that you are not necessarily good at, things you may not enjoy.

I once talked to a bright nineteen year old who absolutely hated school and saw no point to much of the work there. During high school, she never saw the value of classes like history. Once she got in the work place she told me she regretted not trying to learn more during high school. When I asked her why she regretted it, she explained that she often felt stupid in the adult world. She said people around her talked about all kinds of topics that she should have learned about in school, but did not think they were important. This made her feel very uncomfortable and inferior to those around her.

So remember, the point is not algebra. The point is learning how to learn. There are many things you need to learn that you may not like. Just because you don't like them does not mean they are not valuable to you.

BUT I AM A SMART KID, I DON'T NEED ALL THIS STUPID SCHOOL STUFF

I talk to teens all the time who inform me that they are very intelligent and can get by on their intelligence alone. While I do not doubt that many teens are extremely intelligent, I also believe that intelligence alone does not equal success.

In fact, what good is a smart kid without a good education? Colleges do not really care how intelligent you are. They want to know how well you have performed.

Teachers don't give you grades on how intelligent you are, they give you grades on how well you perform.

Bosses really do not care how intelligent you are, they care how you perform. They reward your performance on how hard you work and what you produce, not what you could produce if you tried harder.

It is not one's level of intelligence that determines success.

It is the effort that one is willing to put forth that determines success.

In fact, I know several students who have to work really hard to get B's and C's. I do not worry about these students because I know they will be successful. They will succeed because they are not afraid to work hard, to set goals and to stick with their goals. It is the willingness to do this that determines success.

Ally was a client of mine throughout her high school years. She struggled in school due in part to some serious learning problems. During her first couple years of high school, she put forth very little effort and even talked about dropping out. During her junior year she decided it was time for her to really try, especially in algebra because she had failed it and really needed to pass it in order to graduate. So, for the first time ever, she began to put effort into algebra. She did her homework, studied for tests even asked the resource teacher for help. She was devastated when she got a D-. She told me that she did not mind failing if she had not tried, because then she could tell herself and everyone else, "I could pass it if I tried, I just never cared enough to try." She shared with me that it was much harder to try and fail, and it made her feel even more stupid. However, she did not give up. No miracles here, Ally passed algebra with a D.

When Ally finished high school she enrolled in a very rigorous eighteen month training program to become a licensed aeronautic technician. She did excellent in this program. She told me that 50 people started the program, but only 12 graduated. When I asked her why she thought she was able to stick with it she simply replied, "I think I learned how to do that by never giving up on my algebra class."

The world is full of frustrated, underachieving, unhappy intelligent people.

You have to decide if you are going to be one of these people or if you are willing to insure your success by putting forth effort.

BUT I DON'T LIKE HOMEWORK

I know you do not like homework. Most people don't. That is not the issue.

The issue is whether or not you like the consequences of not doing homework.

Do you like the feeling you get in your gut when report cards come out? Do you like all the lying and evasiveness you have to go through to try and keep your grades from your parents for as long as possible? Do you like thinking about and experiencing your parent's reactions to your grades (their anger, disappointment, and confusion)? Do you like how you feel about yourself when you look at those grades and cannot believe that you are in this situation again? Do you like the worry and concern you have over your future because of your grades? Do you like the consequences of not doing your homework? Do you like not being able to participate in sports or other activities because of your grades? Do you like having to explain this to your friends? Do you like being grounded, not being able to get your license, not being able to get a job, or any of the other restrictions that come because of your grades?

The point is not that you do not like homework. The point is that you need to decide what you dislike

35

most. Do you dislike doing your homework more than you dislike all the consequences that come with not doing your homework?

If you are a typical adolescent, you are thinking a few irrational thoughts that seem to hold the solution to this entire mess.

You might be thinking:

—"My parents should just give up and quit giving me consequences."

—"Teachers should just quit giving us homework."

—"People should not put so much emphasis on stupid grades."

These are indeed nice thoughts. However, they do not solve your problem because they just aren't going to happen.

I once worked with a extremely bright young man named Jim. I met Jim during the summer before his senior year in high school.

Jim did not like to do homework and would rather talk on the phone or spend time with his friends and girlfriend rather than do school work.

Jim had a girlfriend that meant a great deal to him. She was a good student, a serious musician, and was focused on going to college. Jim described her as the kind of girl that most guys would look for when they were ready to select a wife.

Jim had a great time during his first three years of high school. Suddenly, when his senior year came along, things were not so great for him. His girlfriend broke up with him because she felt she wanted a boyfriend with more goals and a better future. His friends were all talking about colleges and visiting campuses. It occurred to Jim that high school was nearing an end and he had few options for himself.

He regretted all the time he wasted having a good time and not thinking about his future.

He worked hard his senior year, but his grades were so poor it did him very little good. He found himself fighting to get into a local community college.

Jim told me, "I thought I hated homework, but I can tell you, I hate how I feel and the situation I am in right now much more than I ever hated homework. I can't believe I did this to myself. How hard could it have been to just study a little?"

Next time you start reminding yourself how much you hate homework, think about all the consequences of not doing homework and ask yourself the question.

What is more of a drag to me, doing my homework or putting up with the consequences of not doing my homework?

You're a smart kid. I'm sure you will make the smart choice.

A WORD FROM MANDY

Mandy is a first semester high school senior who I met during the first nine weeks of her junior year. Mandy came into my office recently excitedly chatting about her grades and college applications.

She was positive and enthusiastic about her future.

We began talking about all that has changed for her during the last year. I reminded her that exactly a year ago she was making failing grades and told me that all she wanted to do was drop out of school. She finds it hard to believe that she not only said that, but she truly believed it at the time. I asked Mandy if she had any words of wisdom for other students struggling with their schoolwork.

Mandy responded, "The future is undefined. Your life is just beginning and no one knows where it will take you. Don't give up on your future so easily, don't screw yourself up so early."

CHAPTER FOUR

So What's In It For Me?

Most kids who struggle with homework and school grades have also been caught in a never ending struggle with their parents, teachers, counselors and many other well meaning and concerned adults. That can be a good thing. It means you have many people in your life concerned about you. Unfortunately (as you know but many adults have not yet figured out) it can also be a problem. It is frustrating to have problems with schoolwork and homework. When you have problems with schoolwork and homework, you end up having a lot of adults all involved in your life and your business. Adults get so involved and concerned with trying to help and trying to solve the problem that it is easy for all involved to forget whose problem homework is. You and I know that it is your problem and you are the only one who can solve it. I am sure you have tried to remind people of this many times.

Unfortunately, when homework and schoolwork becomes a problem focus with your parents, the issue becomes something else all together. It becomes a huge point of conflict and it represents lots of other things.

To begin with, it is a struggle between you trying to assert your independence and your parents trying to assert control. Let's face it, you know you need to do your homework. In fact, you may have days that you actually plan to do your work. Then it happens. That all too familiar voice calls to you.

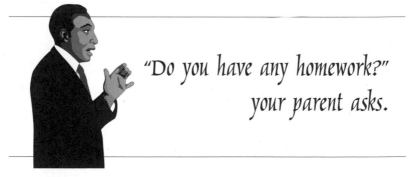

"Do you have any homework?"
your parent asks.

The minute you hear this something snaps inside of you. You grit your teeth and cringe and make up your mind right then and there that you will not do your homework as long as your parents keep nagging you.

You respond with one of your pat answers. "NO!" or the other favorite, "I did it already."

For some strange reason that you and I cannot fathom, your parent does not believe you.

"Are you sure? Let me see it."

Oh great! Now they are really treating you like a stupid baby. You know you don't have it, but even if you did, you would refuse to show it to them.

"It's at school," you reply

We both know what happens next.

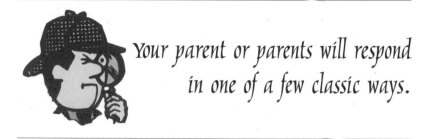

Your parent or parents will respond in one of a few classic ways.

—They will start playing cops and robbers, because they know you don't really have your homework done but they can't prove it, so they will ask you ten million questions to try and trap you to prove that you are lying.

—They will launch into a lecture about your grades, your future, etc. I am sure they are offering you some extremely good advice but you won't really know because you quit listening after the first "You know honey..." that came out of their mouths. You know you should have this lecture memorized because you have heard it no less than a hundred times.

—They begin threatening you, reminding you of the dire punishments which will descend upon you if you bring home another unacceptable report card.

—They shift into their kind and concerned mode and offer to help you, in fact sometimes they beg to help you.

Man, you have to give your parents credit. They are really trying hard. And you know this, but for some reason, the more they help, the more bugged you get. You are frustrated at them because these conversations make you feel like they think you're stupid and incompetent. You are frustrated at yourself because you're so frustrated at them and because you know you ought to have the hang of this homework thing by now.

For some strange reason, this discussion is not about homework.

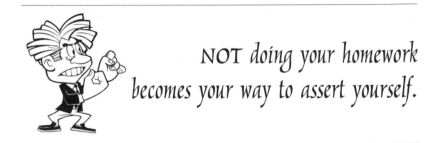

NOT *doing your homework becomes your way to assert yourself.*

It becomes your way of rebelling and pretending that you are taking control of your life. Eventually, you even forget that this discussion is about homework. You dig in your heals and get real stubborn and resolve you will not do your homework and your parents and no one else can make you.

As crazy as this all sounds, it happens to hundreds of teens and parents all over the country. Unfortunately, this becomes a game and it is a game that you can't win because ultimately (as you know) the only person who gets hurt is you.

Not doing your homework and not studying becomes your way of making your parents crazy and giving you a sense of power. Let's face it, it works.

However, you forget that you need to do homework for you. Your parent's lives are already set for them. They may already have good jobs, a nice home, enough money to live comfortably, the satisfaction of knowing that they completed their education. It won't really alter their life one way or the other if you don't do your homework. It will, however, alter the course of your life significantly.

So, forget about making your parents crazy or pick another method. Don't continue to make choices that hurt you because your parents are nagging you.

Focus on getting your homework done by thinking about "What's in this for me? What do I get out of this?"

The answer is simple.

There is a lot in this for you and you will get a lot out of it.

You will feel better about yourself. You will feel good knowing that you set a goal and actually followed through. You will have more confidence in your ability to take charge of your life. You will feel wiser, more mature, and more responsible.

You will not have to live in a constant state of stress going to school everyday knowing that you are not prepared and that it is going to cause problems for you. It takes a lot of energy to think of excuses for your teachers and knowing that they are going to be upset or angry or just give up on you.

You will not have to live in fear of midterms, grade cards, or phone calls home from the teachers.

You will not have to be grounded and restricted from the phone, the car, the computer and everything else you have to live without when your grades are bad.

You will not have to live your life dreading the next lecture from your parents about your grades.

There is a lot in it for you. To help you focus on all that is in this for you, I suggest you get a piece of paper and list everything you have to gain by trying just a little harder with your schoolwork. Give some serious thought to this.

Put the list somewhere where you can see it so it can serve as a reminder to you and keep you motivated.

What's in this for you? That's a very good question.

A WORD FROM ANDY

Andy is a high school sophomore who is a very bright young man who has been diagnosed with Attention Deficit Disorder. His grades have been poor for several years. He always just assumed that once he got to high school, his grades would improve.

He was distressed to discover that his grade point during his freshman year was close to the bottom of his class.

His first grading period during his sophomore year, he made the honor roll. He did it simply by following the same advice I am offering you. When I asked him what was in it for him, his answer was very simple.

"I don't have to be embarrassed when people ask me about my grades."

That is a pretty good reward.

CHAPTER FIVE

So How Do I Get Out of the This Bind I Got Myself Into

I know you really want to make some changes with your schoolwork. I want to offer you a few simple things you can do that will help you significantly. We will keep it short, sweet and practical. If you follow these guidelines, things will get better with you at school.

WHAT TO DO ABOUT TEACHERS

As you know, teachers can make a big difference with your grades. The problem is, students who do not study or do not turn in homework usually have a poor relationship with their teachers. That's because when you do poorly, nice, caring and concerned teachers feel like they have failed, and no one likes to feel that way. This leaves teachers with bad feelings about themselves which often get transferred into bad feelings towards you.

If you do not have a good relationship with your teachers, the first thing you have to do is change that.

Why? Because teachers can be much more helpful and understanding if you have a good relationship with them. Here is what you need to do.

If you have wronged your teacher in any way, apologize. I know you hate to do this but you're going to have a hard time turning your grades around if you and the teacher are locked into a battle.

Explain to your teachers that you have really had a hard time at school and you really want to change that. Ask them if there is anything you can do to get extra credit or make up for some of the poor grades you currently have. They may not have anything, but they will feel much better about you as a student if you ask.

Ask your teachers if they can give you any advice that will help you in their class.

Teachers love to see improvement. They love to reward effort. If they notice you are putting forth more effort, they are much more likely to cut you a few breaks.

Now, a word from the reality section. Most teachers will be great and enthusiastic in helping you. Some will be cranky and cynical. That's life. You have nothing to lose by talking to them and everything to gain. Do It.

PARENTS

We know you have to get things taken care of with your parents. I have included a brief section at the end of this book for parents. Read it and if you decide it will help your cause, ask your parents to read it (what a switch, you asking them to read something).

You definitely need to get out of this power struggle with your parents about your grades and schoolwork. This is the best advice I can give you about your parents.

I want to talk to you about my grades!

Go to your parents and tell them you want to talk to them about your grades.

Be aware that they might faint when you approach this subject with them. After all these years they have been trying to get you to talk to them about your grades.

Find some way to let your parents know that you have heard and understand what their concerns are about your grades. This may prevent you from having to endure future lectures (parents keep repeating lectures because they are just sure you have not heard them). You might want to start this by saying "I know you are worried about my schoolwork and I know _____" Fill in this blank with whatever it is they have been lecturing you about. For example, "I know my grades are poor and I will never get into college if I don't do something to improve them."

Let your parents know how you feel when they nag at you about your grades.

Now let me caution you that this will not go well if you say "You guys make me crazy because you nag me to death and I just want you to shut up about it."

It might go well, however if you say something like "Sometimes I plan to do my work and when you keep reminding me and asking me about it I get stubborn and don't do it. I know that sounds crazy, but I feel like you're treating me like a little kid when you bug me about my homework."

Let your parents know you want to take responsibility for your homework. Come up with a plan (which we will discuss later) and inform them of the plan.

In the future, try to be more honest with your parents about your grades. If you tell your parents you are getting all B's then you bring home D's it is very hard for your parents to deal with that. If you let them know in advance that your grades might not be so great, trust me, it will go much smoother in the long run.

YOUR PLAN

You need to come up with a simple plan for yourself. Here are just a few options.

1. Resolve to put more effort into your homework. As we said before, just start by doing thirty minutes to an hour a day more than you currently do.

 *Learn to reward yourself.*

2. Make a deal with yourself. If you work for just thirty minutes then you will reward yourself by doing something you enjoy. Say to yourself, "After I do just 30 minutes of work, I will go call a friend, shoot some hoops, etc."
3. Keep your attitude about your homework in line. Review Chapter Two and Three and review your list of what is in it for me daily.

4. If you have trouble keeping your work organized, read this. If not skip on to number five.

—Find one place to do your homework.

—When you get home put your book bag in that place.

—Get a folder with a front pocket and a back pocket. Take it to every class with you. When you get worksheets or homework that needs to be done, put it in the front packet of the folder. When you are done with it, place it in back pocket of the folder.

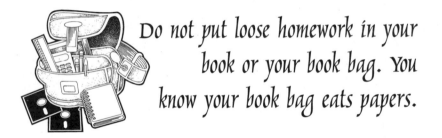

Do not put loose homework in your book or your book bag. You know your book bag eats papers.

—When you are done with your homework put everything back in your book bag.

—Go put the book bag some place you won't forget it. By the front door, in your car, whatever works for you.

—Develop a habit of writing down your assignments in the same place every time. Yes, you have to write down your assignments unless you have a homework hotline you plan to call every night. No, you will not be able to remember them if you do not write them down.

5. If you truly do not understand something at school, get help. Find a friend who can help you. Find a tutor. Ask the teacher for help. No one is good at everything.

HELP!!

It is okay to ask for help.

6. If you are terrible at taking notes, try to find teachers who put their notes on overheads or find a friend who does take good notes and borrow them. Check into tape recording lectures. You don't have to do this for every class, just the ones that you are struggling with because you can't get the notes down.

7. If you have a hard time comprehending or focusing on what you read, read out loud to yourself. It really helps. Another technique that helps is to put a straight edge (like a ruler) above the text that you are reading.

8. If you want to find the quickest way to memorize material so you can spend as little time possible studying, here is what you do. Get a small hand held tape recorder. Read your notes out loud to yourself into the tape recorder. Play the tape back (you could even listen to the tape on the way to school in the morning). By using this technique you see the material, read the material, say the material and hear the material. By using every possible avenue of learning, you will learn the most possible in the shortest period of time.

9. Keep at it. You know you have to learn to study sometime. Today is as good a day as any. It gets easier as time goes on.
10. REMEMBER, school is important, but YOUR WORTH AS A PERSON HAS NOTHING TO DO WITH THE GRADES ON YOUR REPORT CARD!

You may discover you are an awesome student. You may discover you are an average student, but no matter what type of student you are, you are still an important person, so treat yourself that way and get your homework done.

CHAPTER SIX

A Word For Parents

Since you are reading this book I can only assume that you have struggled long and hard to get your darling teen to do his or her homework. Unfortunately, sometimes the harder you try, the worse things get. I often say "Show me an under motivated teen and I'll show you an over motivated parent."

I do not mean to be harsh or critical. I know you have been through a lot of pain and anguish with your adolescent. I have talked to hundreds of parents in the same situation throughout the years.

I hope I can offer some advice in this chapter that is helpful to you. I also hope I can answer some questions for you. Let's start with some questions.

WHY DOES MY TEEN RESIST MY HELP?

It is so hard for well-intentioned parents to understand why teens resist parent's attempts to help them. There are several reasons for this dynamic.

When you remind, nag, lecture, complain, threaten and hover, the schoolwork issue becomes a power struggle. Your teen feels like you think they are stupid and can't handle anything on their own. When you ask your teen if they have any homework to do, they very often decide not to do it. Sometimes they do this to get back at you for nagging. Sometimes they do it to make you crazy. Sometimes they do it to make a point loud and clear that you can't control their lives. Sometimes they resist because if they do their homework after you nag them about it, all the dignity of doing their homework has been taken away.

The last thing teens need is to feel that their parents are responsible for their academic success.

When kids only do homework because you make them, they feel like it is your success and not theirs. That does nothing but hurt the teen's sense of competence and make them doubt themselves. Trust me, they already doubt themselves plenty.

SO WHAT AM I SUPPOSED TO DO? I CAN'T STAND BACK AND DO NOTHING

Your are absolutely right. I would not expect you to stand back and do nothing. That would be irresponsible of you. So we will talk about what you can do and what you cannot do.

To begin with, you have to let go of the notion that you can make your child perform up to his or her potential in school. This is difficult because that means you have to accept the idea that you cannot protect your child from future consequences of his or her poor choices about school.

The truth is, you are an adult and have set your life course. You might be happy with the way things have gone for you and you want similar things for your child.

However, what your child does is really up to him or her.

One of my colleagues tells his sons "I already have a good education, a job I like, and enough money to live comfortably. If you want those things, then you have to do something to get them. If you don't, that's up to you."

You may have struggled as a student yourself and you may regret many of the mistakes you have made. As a result, you may be determined your child will not make the mistakes you made. In reality, it will be your child who decides that and you have to make peace with that reality.

I do not mean you should just pitch all your expectations of your child and let them do whatever they please. I am merely suggesting that your child will ultimately be the one to determine his or her success or failure.

Now, let's talk about what you can do. The solution to the problem lies somewhere between nagging you child to death (which is not effective and not good for either of you) and ignoring him or her.

So, here is my suggestion. I strongly believe that life is very simple. If you want certain things, you have to do certain things. So let your child know what you expect of him or her academically.

I would encourage you to focus more on effort and less on outcome.

I don't know if your child can realistically get all A's and B's. I don't even know if that is really necessary. But I do know your child can complete their homework and study for tests. In other words, they can make more of an effort than they are currently making.

Let them know that you have to see that effort if they expect certain privileges, like driving. Tell them precisely what will happen if they do not put forth that effort.

Set forth a plan for monitoring this effort. With younger teens you can ask for weekly progress updates from teachers. If their weekly progress updates are satisfactory, then they get privileges on the weekend. If not, then they lose privileges that weekend. This provides young teens with short-term rewards and consequences. They respond better to these than long-term rewards.

Let them know you are willing to help them in any way possible and list for them what that entails (a tutor, help with typing research papers, etc.) Tell them that it is their responsibility to ask for that help.

Do not let their problem of poor planning and time management become your problem. For example, you might let them know you will help them type papers, but you will not type after 10:00 at night.

Here is the hard part. Don't say another word to them.

Don't ask them if they have homework, don't warn them about what will happen. LEAVE THEM ALONE.

If they do not live up to the expectations, calmly and without making a big deal about it, enforce the consequences.

BUT WHAT WILL HAPPEN?

To be perfectly honest with you, I am not sure what will happen. Because what happens next is not up to me or to you. It is up to your child.

Many kids respond well just because their parents quit bugging them. Some kids test the system because they don't believe their parents will stick with the consequences.

Many kids realize if their schoolwork is going to improve, they will have to do it because mom and dad are no longer going to take responsibility.

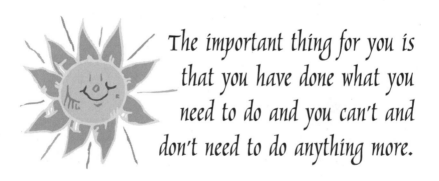

The important thing for you is that you have done what you need to do and you can't and don't need to do anything more.

The rest is up to your child. I have seen many parents who report that they have tried the hands-off approach and it failed. When I asked how it failed, they report that their teen's grades just got worse. This is where I remind parents that if you set expectations, monitor expectations, and provide appropriate consequences, you have not failed. You have been a good and responsible parent. The failure belongs to the child. If your child stops functioning academically the minute you stop drilling him or her, it is clear that your child has become way too dependent on you. This dependence will hurt your child in the short and long run. It's time to do something about this. That something is to let them take responsibility.

I have known many teens who feel they do not have to take responsibility because they know their parents will step in and take control of the situation. This enables the teens to be irresponsible and lazy.

Parents have to ask themselves to examine their goals for their children.

Is the goal to just get the teen out of high school? Or is the goal to produce a responsible, functioning adult?

Many teens do make it through high school and even to college only because their parents hounded them relentlessly about their grades. However, once faced with the challenges of college, they failed miserably because they were not prepared. Many drop out or flunk out of college and fail miserably in the workforce as well.

Unfortunately, many parental efforts to help our kids often cripples them in the areas that truly count.

A FEW WORDS ABOUT YOUR RELATIONSHIP WITH YOUR TEEN

Many times the worst thing about teens getting poor grades is the impact this has on your relationship with them. I have had many teens tell me that all their parents ever talk to them about is their grades. They hate this—especially if teens view this as a negative subject.

Your teen is a person as well as a student.

Be aware that they do not want to talk endlessly about the thing that they think is causing them the most problems in their life. Do not get stuck in a conflict with your child about his or her grades. Stay balanced in your approach with them. Quit telling them how you feel about their grades and start asking them how they feel. Quit telling them how they are going to solve the problem and start asking them how they are going to solve the problem.

Most importantly, don't let your attitude about their school performance become your attitude about them. Talk to your teen about other more pleasant things.

The reality is that most adolescents "Get it" eventually. Certainly, the sooner they get it, the easier their lives will be. However, you cannot protect them from the long-term consequences of their choices. If your child wakes up at some point in the future and decides they want to get a good education, there are several options available to them. They may have to put forth a great deal of effort to access these options.

For most teens, poor school performance is a detour, not a dead end street.

It is a detour which your child will have to navigate and endure. You cannot do it for them.

BUT WHAT ABOUT MY CHILD'S SELF ESTEEM?

Very often, parents are overinvolved in their child's schoolwork because they are concerned that not performing well in school will damage their child's self-esteem. If your child is not performing well in school because there is an obstacle to your child's learning, then poor school performance may in fact, become a self-esteem problem. Obstacles to learning are possibly learning disabilities, emotional problems (such as depression, or anxiety), problems with paying attention, and stress. If you suspect these are issues, contact your child's school counselor and asks for a recommendation on having your child evaluated. With proper diagnosis and treatment, your child can learn to compensate for, or overcome these obstacles.

If your child's school performance is simply a result of your child not putting forth effort into his or her work, you cannot ward off poor self-esteem by becoming overly involved. In fact, when parents are overly involved, it actually hurts teens' self-esteem. It gives them the message that they are incompetent to take care of themselves. Most teens fear that this is true. They are afraid they are not smart enough, mature enough, or responsible enough to take care of themselves. Every time you remind them they are not responsible or mature you tap into their worse fear and they will respond to you with deep hostility. Every time you do something for them that they can do for themselves, you confirm for them that they cannot take care of themselves.

Once again, they will respond with deep hostility.

Let them know you know they are smart, and capable of making mature and responsible decisions. This is why you have set expectations and consequences. All you can do now is sit back and patiently wait for them to demonstrate their maturity. Kick back and try to enjoy life in the meantime, because this might take a little while.

APPENDIX

Tips for Test Taking

Test taking is a skill. Like any other skill, it can be learned and it can be mastered. Review the following tips that will help you with test taking. Some of these you may already know and use. Others will be new to you. If you are doubtful that these will help, just pick one or two and see what happens.

TECHNIQUES FOR SUCCEEDING DURING TEST TAKING SITUATIONS INCLUDE THE FOLLOWING:

- —Read the directions carefully. It may help to underline the directions if at all possible.
- —Complete sample questions if offered.
- —Begin as soon as you are instructed to.

—If you are concerned about forgetting particular facts, you might want to jot these down in pencil somewhere on the test as soon as the test is passed to you.

—Skim the test to get a feel for the time you think you might need.

—Budget your time and don't spend all your time on a part of the test you do not know.

—If you freeze up, go on and answer the questions you do know.

—If you feel you are spending too much time on a particular section or question, skip it and come back to it later.

—If you have any say about where you sit, select your seating carefully.

-Avoid sitting by windows and isles.
-Do not sit close to the door.
-Do not sit close to friends or acquaintances that might distract you.

—Do not allow yourself to become distracted by others finishing the test before you do.

MASTERING MULTIPLE CHOICE TESTS:

—Be attentive. Pay attention to what you are doing and reading. Read each word. One word in the question or in an answer can completely change the meaning.

—If you are not sure of an answer, skip the question and come back to it.

When you skip a question, flag it so it will be easy to find.

—Read all directions carefully.

—Read the sentence carefully. Pay close attention to words that may make a difference in the answer.

—After reading the question, try to guess the answer before you read the choices. This will help you be more confident and less likely to get confused by the other answers offered.

—If the correct answer does not appear to be on the list, select the answer which is closest.

—Eliminate the incorrect answers in the following order: obviously wrong answers, partially wrong answers, and answers which are correct statements but which have nothing to do with the question (these are sometimes the trickiest).

—When two answers seem correct and are very similar, try to determine in what ways the answers are different and how that difference makes one of them correct and one of them incorrect.

—If you do not know the answer, look for familiar phrases.

—Skip a question if you do not know the answer and look for clues in the questions that follow.

—If you do not understand the wording of a question, try to replace abstract words with more concrete words, then attempt to answer the question.

—Utilize your time well.

—After you have taken the test, go back and answer the questions you skipped.

—If you still do not know the answer, guess.

The best way to guess is to narrow down the two most probable answers and select one.

—After completing the questions you left blank, go back and review each question and answer.

THE FOLLOWING TIPS WILL HELP YOU DEAL WITH TEST ANXIETY:

—Stop worrying about worrying. Test anxiety is normal and will not prevent you from doing well on the test. Test anxiety becomes a problem when you worry that you are so anxious you will not do well. So quit convincing yourself you have test anxiety and focus your thoughts on the fact that you are prepared.

If you are not prepared, freaking out about it won't help you now.

• Anxiety usually starts with a thought and ends up in a physical reaction which includes not breathing correctly. If you want to enhance your concentration while studying and stay calm during a test follow this routine:

- Before studying for a test close your eyes. Take three deep breathes (in through your nose, all the way into your stomach, out through your mouth).

- Before you take the test, repeat the breathing. It will help you calm down as well as recall the information you know.

—Do not let your thoughts get negative and get the best of you. Instead of saying, "I'm so stupid, I know I'm going to flunk" remind yourself, "I know this well enough to pass it."

—Make sure you have prepared your body as well as your mind. Make sure you get enough sleep, avoid a lot of junk food the day before the test and eat something decent the day of the test.

We know that your mind and body work together.

—If you have a learning disability or have been diagnosed with attention deficit disorder, you have a right to certain considerations during a test. Here are some of the things that might help you.

  -Ask for extra time to take the test.

  -Take the test in the resource room or in a room that is quiet and with fewer distractions.

  -If you are able to take the test in a room by yourself, read the questions out loud to yourself. This will help insure you don't overlook or misread words.

  -Utilize whatever help that has been offered to you.

BIBLIOGRAPHY

Gifford, Charles S., and John L. Fluitt, Test Taking Made Easier, The Interstate Printers and Publishers Inc., Danville, IL 1981

Kesselman-Turkel and Franklynn Peterson, Test Taking Strategies, Contemporary Books Inc. Chicago, IL 1981.

PROFESSIONAL RESOURCE PUBLICATIONS
P.O. BOX 501485 • INDIANAPOLIS, INDIANA 46256
317-465-9688 • 317-465-9689 (FAX)
www.newsperspectives-indy.com

ORDER FORM

THE FOLLOWING MATERIAL BY JANICE GABE, MSW, CCSW, NCAC II, IS AVAILABLE:

VIDEOTAPES: *"IS IT ADOLESCENCE OR PATHOLOGY?"*
___ $50 - ($5.95 S&H for 1, $3 each additional tape)

CULTURES OF CHANGE - see below ($5.95 S&H for 1, $9.95 for all)
___ Tape 1 - "Parenting in Cultures of Change" 1 tape: $30.00
___ Tape 2 - "Value Based Parenting" 2 tapes: $60.00
___ Tape 3 - "Value Based Discipline" 3 tapes: $90.00

AUDIOTAPES: $7.00 EACH PLUS 75 ¢ SHIPPING CHARGE PER PAMPHLET
___ *VALUE BASED PARENTING*
___ *VALUE BASED CONSEQUENCES*

BOOKS: (PRICED AS MARKED) SEE SHIPPING CHARGE BELOW
___ *A PROFESSIONALS GUIDE TO DUAL DISORDERS* - $17.00 EA.
___ *CULTURES OF CHANGE: RECOVERY AND RELAPSE PREVENTION FOR DUALLY DIAGNOSED AND ADDICTED ADOLESCENTS* - $12.95 EACH
___ *MAKING THE GRADE: THE TEEN'S GUIDE TO HOMEWORK SUCCESS* - $7.95

** BOOK SHIPPING CHARGE IS $2.00 FOR THE FIRST BOOK
   AND 75¢ FOR EACH ADDITIONAL BOOK

THE FOLLOWING MATERIAL BY JAMES KEYES, MA, CCSW, MAC, IS AVAILABLE:

PAMPHLET: $3.00 EACH PLUS 75 CENTS SHIPPING CHARGE PER PAMPHLET
___ ADOLESCENT SUBSTANCE ABUSE: A GUIDE FOR PARENTS
   AND PROFESSIONALS

* INDIANA RESIDENTS ALSO INCLUDE 5% SALES TAX
* A 20% RESTOCK FEE WILL BE ASSESSED FOR ANY RETURNED MATERIALS

NAME: _____

ADDRESS: _____

_____

TELEPHONE: _____

___ CHECK   ___ VISA   ___ MASTERCARD   ___ AMERICAN EXPRESS

CARD NUMBER_____
SIGNATURE (REQUIRED FOR CREDIT CARD)

75

ABOUT THE AUTHOR

Janice Gabe is the founder and president of New Perspectives of Indiana, a counseling, consultation and training corporation.

Ms. Gabe has 20 years of experience working with children, adolescents and families. She has lectured extensively throughout the country and has provided keynote addresses at treatment, prevention, parenting, and school-based conferences. Ms. Gabe is recognized as one of the country's leading experts in the needs and issues facing kids and families.

Ms. Gabe is the author of *Value Based Parenting, Value Based Consequences, Cultures of Change: Recovery and Relapse Prevention for Dually Diagnosed and Addicted Adolescents, Professional Guide to Dual Disorders in Adolescents.*

In addition, Ms. Gabe has published a series of videotapes and audiotapes. They are as follows:

<u>Videotape</u>
Is it Adolescence of Pathology?

<u>Videotape</u>
3-Part Series: Parenting in Cultures of Change

<u>Audiotape</u>
Parenting in Cultures of Change

<u>Audiotape</u>
Celebrating the Kindergarten Child